COMPASS

Discerning Your Calling

DISCOVER YOUR PLACE AS A GLOBAL WORKER

JOHN WARD

D0916621

V1-0618

Discerning your Calling
Discover Your Place as a Global Worker

© 2018 Encompass World Partners
ISBN: 978-0-9978640-9-0
Published by Encompass World Publishing, Atlanta, GA 30362
the publishing arm of Encompass World Partners
EncompassWorldPartners.org

Written by John Ward
Edited by John Ward, Cody Irwin, Evangela Creative, Bill Palmateer
Design and Layout by Evangela Creative (evangela.com)

Printed in U.S.A.

ABOUT THE SERIES

THE PATH: NAVIGATING THE JOURNEY TO GLOBAL MISSIONS

Travel tools and resources help us learn about destinations, give us insights, and point the way. Likewise, the titles in this series act as a map, a guide, and a compass to help you navigate the journey to global missions.

Start down the path to knowing God's heart for the nations and how you can become a part of his global mission.

Next steps on the path for those who are mobilizing individuals and teams into meaningful ministry to the nations.

Next steps on the path for potential cross-cultural workers discerning the call to make disciples among the nations.

ABOUT THE AUTHOR

JOHN WARD has served in mobilization with Encompass World Partners since 2007. In his current role as the Director of Mobilization, he's passionate about connecting and mobilizing a diverse group of people and churches who follow Jesus in the work to make disciples of all nations. John is a graduate of *Cedarville University*, where he studied broadcasting and business. Shortly after John and his wife, Kate, were married, they served on a disciple-making team that reached out primarily to college students in London, England. John and Kate, together with their three boys, live among the ethnically diverse neighborhoods of Northeast Atlanta, where they are seeking to plant churches.

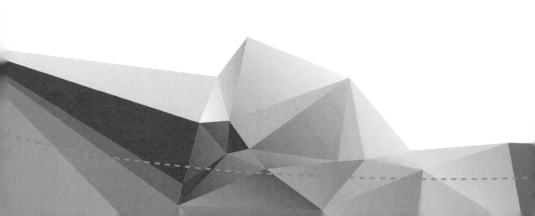

ABOUT THE AGENCY

ENCOMPASS WORLD PARTNERS was birthed in 1900 from a commitment to make disciples among all nations.

Its purpose is: To mobilize, equip, deploy and nurture multinational teams of disciple-makers who live and proclaim the good news of Jesus Christ through engaging in sacrificial service, intentional evangelism and whole-life discipleship, resulting in the creation of healthy spiritual communities (churches).

The rallying cry of Encompass World Partners is *more fruitful disciple-making teams among the least-reached peoples of our world*. Learn more about the ministries of Encompass and how you can become involved at EncompassWorldPartners.org.

TABLE OF CONTENTS

INTRODUCTION
WHAT IS GOD CALLING ME TO DO?

That's a question we all ask ourselves. We pray about it and wrestle with it. Sometimes it even keeps us up at night.

This is especially true if you believe God may be calling you to cross-cultural ministry. I'm glad you've given us the opportunity to be a small part of your journey to discover your God-given calling.

The truth is, God has a plan and purpose for your life, and he has given you everything you need to accomplish his will. Furthermore, he's not calling you to go alone—he promises to be with you every step of the way. In Psalm 139:1–3, David says, "O Lord, you have searched me and known me! You know when I sit down and when I rise up; you discern my thoughts from afar. You search out my path and my lying down and are acquainted with all my ways."

As you seek to discern your calling, you can't know what the future will hold, but you can know with confidence the One who holds your future, and you can trust him. This certain hope is confirmed through the words of the apostle Paul: "For we are his workmanship, created in Christ Jesus for good works, which God prepared beforehand, that we should walk in them" (Ephesians 2:10).

We live in an age of infinite options and immediate results. We are accustomed to finding answers to our questions through a simple Google search or by asking Siri. The convenience and efficiency of these tools are great when you need to know where to go to dinner or what the weather is like in Bolivia, but they are no substitute for the lifelong process of seeking God and asking what he wants to do through your life.

My hope is that this book will not only convince you of the importance of your primary calling to God, but will also help you with practical steps in discerning a vocational calling to serve in cross-cultural ministry. Before we go any further, let's define our terms.

CLARIFYING DEFINITIONS

In his book *Gaining by Losing: Why the Future Belongs to Churches that Send*, J. D. Greear points out that many who are asking the question of calling are waiting for the voice of God but forgetting that we already have his will spelled out in the Great Commission. He writes, "We shouldn't be waiting on a voice when we already have verses." [1] Jesus commands each of his followers to go and make disciples of all nations. Greear writes, "The question is no longer if we are called to leverage our lives for the Great Commission, only where and how." [2] In an effort to bust the myth of calling, Greear's church holds to a powerful conviction—one that challenges every believer:

> "Whatever you're good at, do it well for the glory of God, and do it somewhere strategic for the mission of God." [3]

Os Guinness provides some nuance to these ideas in his book *The Call: Finding and Fulfilling the Central Purpose of Your Life*. Guinness lays out two distinct types of calling: "Our primary calling as followers of Christ is by him,

[1] J. D. Greear, *Gaining By Losing: Why the Future Belongs to Churches that Send* (Grand Rapids: Zondervan, 2015), 78, 79.
[2] Ibid., 78.
[3] Ibid., 75

to him, and for him. First and foremost we are called to Someone (God), not to something (such as motherhood, politics, or teaching) or to somewhere (such as the inner city or Outer Mongolia)… Our secondary calling, considering who God is as sovereign, is that everyone, everywhere, and in everything should think, speak, live, and act entirely for him." [4]

Guinness later says, "A sense of calling should precede a choice of job and career, and the main way to discover calling is along the line of what we are each created and gifted to be." [5] Guinness's admonition to make sure that Christ is in his rightful place as Lord of our lives will help us not make an idol of our work.

One of my favorite quotes from the book is in reference to the gifts God has given each of us to steward: "The truth is not that God is finding us a place for our gifts but that God has created us and our gifts for a place of His choosing, and we will only be ourselves when we are finally there." [6] In other words, our gifts and abilities are from God and should rightfully be used for his purposes. When we align our gifts with his will, we will find our calling and our joy.

The number one reason people serve as missionaries is because they have an inner conviction to walk in obedience to a calling from God. This idea is developed by the great modern American missiologist Ralph D. Winter, who claims that Paul and his missionary counterparts from the Antioch church experienced a second decision or second conversion before they were sent out as missionaries. The Holy Spirit said, "set apart for me Barnabas and Saul for the work to which I have called them" (Acts 13:2). Winter argues that the call to cross-cultural ministry is experienced as a second call, subsequent to our call to follow Jesus.

The focus of this book is that second decision to serve in cross-cultural ministry. The principles can be applied to anyone seeking answers to the

[4] Os Guinness, The Call (Nashville: 2003), 31.
[5] Ibid., 45.
[6] Ibid., 46.

questions of calling, but it is primarily intended to be a helpful resource for those who are discerning God's call to serve as global workers or missionaries.

The definition of calling that we'll be working from is:

> *"God's call is an inner conviction given by and through the Holy Spirit and confirmed by the Word of God, the body of Christ, and the character of the called."* [7]
>
> **Ryan Johnston**

There are a couple things to observe in this definition. First note that God works through the Holy Spirit, his Word, and his Church to confirm a calling. It is the agreement of these three sources that assures we are hearing the voice of God. Second, calling never outpaces the character of the person called. In other words, godly character is the foundation of a God-given calling; you can't have true calling where there is no godly character.

ADDRESSING MISCONCEPTIONS

Before we move ahead, I'd like to clear up a few potential misconceptions. First of all, the call to missions is not only for those who serve on the frontlines of cross-cultural missions. The Great Commission is not only for God's global workers—it is for every follower of Christ. Every Christian has an important role to play in God's global mission to make disciples of all nations. The first book in The Path Series, *Discovering Global Missions*, identifies the roles of praying, giving, going, and welcoming. Every job and every worker is equally important in the spread of God's Kingdom.

Secondly, we need to assert that God's economy is totally different from the world's economy. If you use the world's blueprint for success, you might miss out on the very things God wants to accomplish through you. This is a call to die to yourself, to put your life in God's hands, and to live by faith. The pursuit of a God-given calling isn't about being successful in the world's eyes. In fact, chances are that following his call will look foolish to the world.

[7] Ryan Johnston, *Examining the "Call" to Ministry* (theHSF.com: 2011)

ORIENTING DIRECTIONS

You may have heard it said, "It's easier to steer a moving ship." Similarly, you can't arrive at a destination if you're not taking active steps along the path to get there. I hope this book will help you launch in the direction of your calling. As you prepare to start this journey, you need a few orienting directions to help you keep your bearings. We've named this tool in The Path Series *The Compass* because these bearings represent the directions of north, south, east, and west.

UPWARD // **God Awareness:** Knowing and loving God is our primary calling, and we can't discover our secondary calling if God is not the Lord of our lives. He is our true north, the One who is the way and shows us the way. Without the leading of God's Spirit, we will not be able to hear and respond to his call for our lives.

INWARD // **Self-Awareness:** God has given each of us unique gifts and abilities, and these are best utilized when we are aware of what they are and how we can use them to build up the body of Christ. The higher our level of self-awareness is, the greater the chances that we will find the right fit in ministry.

OUTWARD // **Cultural Awareness:** We need to understand our cultural context in order to know how to communicate the gospel. Jesus used an agricultural metaphor to illustrate this (Matthew 13). In this story the soil represents the culture, and the seed is not only the Bible, but also us. If we are going to effectively plant ourselves in the diverse cultural soils of this world, we need to understand the culture we are serving, especially if we are called to cross-cultural ministry.

FORWARD // **Movement Awareness:** Remember Newton's First Law of Motion? An object at rest stays at rest, but an object in motion stays in motion. Simply put you can't arrive at your destination without taking the next step forward. Discerning your calling, just like the Christian life, is a journey and there's always a next step. Each step you take, big or small, can create forward motion that leads to movement toward your destination.

FINAL INSTRUCTIONS

I'm so glad you've accessed this book, and I pray that it will help you discover the unique role God is calling you to pursue in his global mission. I've formatted the book for learning, reflection, and guidance. Each chapter covers an important next step in the journey, a *Digging Deeper* section with questions to consider and Scripture to meditate on, plus a *Called* story from people we've journeyed with.

The journey to discern your calling is best supported by a local mentor who will pray and process with you. I encourage you to seek out a spiritual leader from your church who can engage with you as you read the book and who will continue with you in the journey to discern your calling.

Finally, the mobilization team at Encompass World Partners is here to help you take the next steps in your journey. We connect and mobilize a diverse group of people and churches who follow Jesus in his work of making disciples of all nations. We are committed to investing in you personally and professionally so you're prepared for a fruitful, growing ministry. We'd love to talk to you about your calling to God's global mission. For more information, visit **EncompassWorldPartners.org/GO.** ●

CHAPTER 1

IN SEARCH OF ANSWERS

THE MOMENT YOU GAVE YOUR LIFE TO CHRIST, YOU GAINED A NEW PURPOSE.

As the apostle Paul put it, "I have been crucified with Christ; and it is no longer I who live, but Christ lives in me; and the life which I now live in the flesh I live by faith in the Son of God, who loved me and gave Himself up for me" (Galatians 2:20). If you have made Jesus the Lord of your life, you live no longer for yourself but for him. It is no longer your passions and desires that rule in your heart, but God's.

The question is, how will that shape your life? As Director of Mobilization with Encompass World Partners, I hear this question frequently. It is often worded like this: "What is God calling me to do? How can I tell the difference between God's calling and my own desires? With so many ministry opportunities, and limited hours in the day, how do I discern which ones I should pursue?" All good questions, and none of them are easily answered.

Of course, there are some fundamental answers to the question of God's call that apply to all believers. God is calling you to pursue a vibrant, intimate relationship with him. He is calling you to a life of obedience to the Bible's commands and loving care for others. And he is calling you to fulfill the Great Commission, making disciples of all nations. If you are walking with Jesus, these are your primary goals in life, just as they are for every believer.

But the question remains, what specific role does God have for you in his Kingdom? Where does your calling meet the world's need? Where do your gifts and opportunities intersect with the deepest need of others, to know and respond to the love of Jesus?

SOLVING THE MYSTERY

This idea of calling is somewhat of a mystery, but it's a mystery God is intent on helping you solve. If you desire to serve him with your life, he will show you how to do it. And he will guide you in a way that is unique to the way he has made you.

Consider how God called people in the Bible. Not everyone had a burning bush experience like Moses, a moment where God told them straight-out in an audible voice what he wanted them to do. Isaiah offered himself when he saw God in his holiness—he was so overwhelmed by what he saw that he couldn't help himself. Amos was already well into his career as a shepherd when he was called. Samuel was called when he was a young boy serving in the Temple, whereas Paul was called later in life while in the act of persecuting Christians. When we look at the type of people God called and how he made his calling known in the Bible, there is no observable pattern. God called people from all walks of life, at all ages, in many different ways.

It is no different in our age; the spectrum of experience seems to have just as much variety today. It would be nice if God wrote his plan for you in the sky, but that hasn't been the experience of anyone I know. There are no 12-step programs or proven formulas that promise results in just two weeks.

Sadly, many people expect the answers to these life questions in an instant, the same way they are accustomed to receiving answers through a Google search. The truth is, God has an amazing, fantastic, wonderful plan for your life, and he will be faithful to his promise to complete the work he has begun in you. But the answers to the specific what and how questions will come on his timetable, not yours, and God is never in a hurry.

"God's call is an inner conviction given by and through the Holy Spirit and confirmed by the Word of God, the body of Christ, and the character of the called." [7]

Ryan Johnston

GPS-GOD'S POSITIONING SYSTEM

Instead of bemoaning the lack of a burning bush in your life, consider what God *has* given you. God has not left you alone in this search for life purpose and calling—he has a three-part positioning system to help you orient yourself to the role he has for you in fulfilling the Great Commission.

First, he's given you the Holy Spirit as a guide, a supernatural helper who will never leave you alone as you journey through life. This is the comforter and guide Jesus said was even better than having the Son of God present in bodily form (John 16:7). The inner promptings of the Holy Spirit are crucial to hearing and responding to God's call.

In addition, God has given his Word as light for your path, illuminating the way before you as you seek him. When you study it each day, you will find wisdom for all of life's decisions, big and small. The Bible is God's living and active word to you, the source of life and light that will teach you and train you in righteousness (2 Timothy 3:16).

Finally, the body of Christ assures that you don't have to go alone. You have brothers and sisters, fathers and mothers in the faith to journey with you and point out signposts along the way. They will confirm the gifts they see in you and warn you when you're getting off track. As with any journey, the path to discovering your life's calling is more enjoyable with traveling companions. So, don't try to go it alone; make use of the friends and fellow travelers God provides.

[7] Ryan Johnston, *Examining the "Call" to Ministry* (theHSF.com; 2011)

As you make use of these gifts God has provided to help you discern your calling, your faithful pursuit of God through the ups and downs of life will give you even greater confidence in both your calling and the One who has called you.

DO THE NEXT THING

Most of the people I encounter are at the beginning of their journey to discern God's call for missions, and they fear that they are going to get it wrong. They are suffering from what I call analysis paralysis, option fatigue, or some combination of both. With so many opportunities available, they can't seem to choose one. Either they over-analyze themselves and their circumstances, paralyzing themselves, or they simply refuse to make a decision amongst the options available to them. They are so terrified of getting it wrong that they don't do anything.

If that's where you find yourself, let me offer the encouragement that God has not given us a spirit of fear, but rather a spirit of freedom in his Son (2 Timothy 1:7). Ask God to grow your faith in him and what he has promised, and he will.

The best advice I can give you is to do the next thing. Your job isn't to figure it all out now, but to take the step God has laid before you today. He knows where the path is leading, and you can trust him to get you there. But don't expect him to show you the final destination at the beginning. In fact, chances are good that if you knew everything he is calling you to, you'd be too scared to even begin. God hasn't yet prepared you for the final destination, only for the next step. In his mercy, God reveals his will one step at a time so that all you have to do is the next thing.

The reality is, if you're putting your trust in God and obediently following him, it's impossible to get it wrong. Rather than fearing that you're going to miss God's will, pursue him. It's when you take your eyes off Jesus that you lose sight of the path he's called you to. But if you seek God and pursue an understanding of how he has uniquely gifted you, you will find the answers to your questions about calling. That's what David meant when he wrote, "Take delight in the Lord, and he will give you the desires of your heart" (Psalm 37:4).

THE GOAL: YOUR SWEET SPOT

Although we can't know the final step until we get there, it is helpful to know what we're aiming for. As we try to discover our calling, what we are really looking for is our "sweet spot." *This* is the place where we say, "Aha, this is what I was made to do!" The "SWEET SPOT" is the intersection of our passions, abilities, and opportunities, all within the sphere of what others have affirmed in us. I like to diagram it this way:

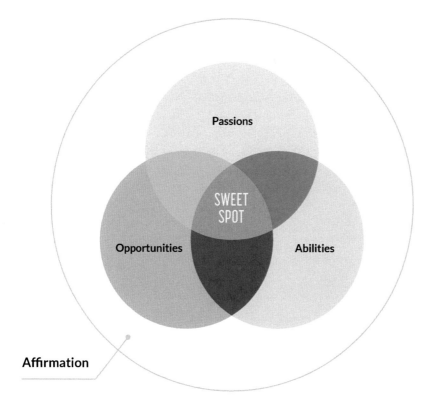

God motivates and prepares his people for ministry through the desires, opportunities, and abilities he gives. Think of the last time you felt totally in tune with both God and yourself. Some people call this "flow," that moment when you were doing some sort of ministry and totally lost track of time because it was actually fun. Or think of the time when you had an opportunity to do something and thought, "Yes, I can definitely do that—and I can't wait to get started!" When was the last time someone told you, "You're really good at that, you should do more of it"? These are all signs pointing you to your sweet spot.

As you trust God to guide you on this journey to discover your calling, being honest with yourself and seeking the input of those who know you well will help you more confidently step into your "sweet spot." Don't give answers that you think are "right" to please someone else, or say things that you wish were true of you; answer truthfully so that you can find God's path for you.

God has a job for you to do, and it perfectly suits the way he made you—your temperament, talents, loves, and life experiences. The things you learn about yourself as you uncover your passions, abilities, and opportunities are the clues that will help you solve the mystery behind the question of calling.

 DIGGING DEEPER

Questions to Consider

1. What are your deepest passions in life? What are the inner motivations that move you to take action, the things you are interested in or issues that are close to your heart?

2. What are your God-given abilities? What are your strengths, spiritual gifts, or natural talents?

3. What opportunities would you like to explore? Maybe there's an opportunity that's right in front of you; consider it with these other factors in mind.

4. Finally, seek the affirmation of those who know you well. What are your close friends, family, mentors, and church leaders saying about all of the above?

Scriptures to Consider

As you think about your passions, abilities, opportunities, and affirmations, read the passages listed below and meditate on how God called people in the Bible. What principles about calling can you learn from these stories?

> Exodus 3:10–14; Isaiah 6:8; 1 Samuel 3; Amos 7:15; Jeremiah 20:9;
> John 15:16; Matthew 4:19; Acts 9

CALLED: PREPARED, BROKEN, AND SENT

While visiting the country of her childhood, Claire was captured by an idea she had long ago dismissed, an idea that now would not let her go.

The preparation had begun many years before. Claire's parents met while serving at the Chateau of Saint-Albain, France. They were married in the States but always planned to return to the country where they fell in love. In 1992, they traveled back to France as long-term missionaries with nine-month-old Claire in tow.

Though Claire loved growing up in France, the quest for self-discovery was hard.

She did not fully relate to the culture of her parents, and she did not fully identify with the culture in which she was living. She found herself in the place of in-between; a culture of her own. For a time it was a place of not-belonging, but eventually Claire anchored herself in the reality of this "third culture." She was a Missionary Kid (MK). This was how she wanted the world to see her, and how she saw herself.

After embracing this identity, Claire grew to fully appreciate it. She lived in a beautiful country, she was well-traveled, and she was able to speak two languages. Having found peace in who she was, Claire built her whole world around her identity as an MK.

Then, on Easter Sunday when she was 16 years old, her world collapsed.

The Martins gathered Claire and her younger siblings into the living room for an important announcement: They were going to leave France and move back to the United States.

Claire's heart sank. She would rather live in a jungle or in a place where Christians are persecuted for their faith than move to the US. She was willing to go anywhere, as long as her parents would still be missionaries. She was a Missionary Kid, and that meant she lived in an exotic place while her parents did full-time ministry. If they moved to America, what would that make her?

Who was she without the label of MK?

When the Martins moved to Colorado Springs, Claire became immensely depressed and angry with God. Though she still had faith, it was hard for her to fully trust the God who had ripped everything away from her.

It took three years for her trust to return.

In her college years, Claire began to accept that God's plans were better than hers. She finally saw the reason God pulled her out of the identity she had grown too comfortable with, the one that was becoming an idol. She realized that she needed to build her identity on Christ alone, not on what she or her parents did for him.

As she came to terms with who she was as a child of God, Claire felt like she needed to reach closure on her previous life. In order to say goodbye to France, Claire and a friend flew to Europe before their last year of college. One of the stops they made was the Chateau of Saint-Albain, where her parents first met.

While staying at the Chateau, Claire had the opportunity to help out with daily tasks for the ministry. It all came so easily for her. She knew the people, the culture, and the language. As she realized how natural it was for her to serve at the Chateau, Claire had a thought she never imagined she would have.

I could work here.

Claire had vowed as a young girl that she would never become a missionary, so even considering that possibility was astonishing. She had a job she liked back at home, and friends she enjoyed. Why would she leave all that? Had God brought her to this point, only to completely redirect her? It didn't make sense. For a time Claire wrestled with the idea, but in the end, she couldn't escape the fact that God had been preparing her for this ministry her whole life.

God used a lifetime of experiences and abilities to prepare Claire for ministry in France, broke her self-made identity to help her depend on him, and put her together again to fulfill the work he called her to. Claire now serves full-time at the Chateau, focusing on outreach to youth, and she is delighted to be living in France once again.

CHAPTER 2

PRAYER, VISION, PASSION

IMAGINE I GAVE YOU A RECIPE FOR HOW TO MAKE A DELICIOUS CAKE THAT YOU REALLY CRAVED, BUT I DIDN'T GIVE YOU ANY INGREDIENTS.

I'm guessing your next move would be to go find the ingredients—that is, if you really wanted to "have your cake and eat it too." (Sorry, I couldn't resist.)

In the last chapter, I offered a recipe for calling. I gave you a definition to work from and some helpful indicators to help you discern your calling. But I withheld the ingredients of calling—until now. The three ingredients of calling are prayer, vision, and passion. Let's take a look at each one.

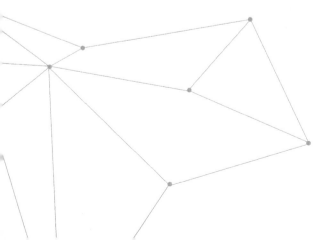

..

PRAYER

Prayer is the basis for calling. It is the foundation upon which it rests and the lifeblood from which it springs. D.L. Moody once said, "Some people think God doesn't like to be troubled with our constant coming and asking, [but] the way to trouble God is not to come at all." We can't know our God-given calling unless we ask God in prayer and listen to his answers.

At its heart, choosing not to pray or talk to God about your calling is assuming the role of God. You are telling God and the world that you can figure this out on your own, without his input. The end result of this kind of arrogance is that you will miss out, because God's ways are always higher than ours. Tom Julien, Director Emeritus of Encompass World Partners, in his article about prayer called "Thoughts on Intercession," writes, "When we assume the role of God, we rule over a pitifully small kingdom. When we take our place in Christ at the right hand of God, we move our lives into His great plan." God's ideas are often bigger—and always better—than ours.

If you are leaving prayer out of your journey to discern God's calling and purpose for your life, then it is safe to say that you haven't truly made him Lord of your life. Consider how God addressed King Solomon and the Israelites on this matter:

> If my people who are called by my name humble themselves, and pray and seek my face and turn from their wicked ways, then I will hear from heaven and will forgive their sin and heal their land.

2 Chronicles 7:14

Those who have truly bowed their hearts before God in humble admission of their sin will want to pray about what concerns them. It is convicting and sobering to realize the extent of our arrogance toward God if we claim to have a calling from him but have not asked him about it through prayer. God holds the answers to all of our questions, but he wants us to seek him in prayer before he'll answer. Look at how James reveals this in the first chapter of his letter.

If any of you lacks wisdom, let him ask God, who gives generously to all without reproach, and it will be given him.

James 1:5

James goes on to say that we must believe and not doubt. Do you believe God wants to give you wisdom to discern your calling? Ask him for wisdom and know that he wants to give it generously. No journey to discern your calling can happen without the first and most important ingredient of prayer. As D. L. Moody once said, "Every great movement of God can be traced back to a kneeling figure."

VISION

Discerning your calling is going to take a little bit of outside-the-box creative thinking. If you stick to only the things you've already done or seen someone else do, you may miss the new things God is calling you to. I call this vision—the ability to hope for a positive future outcome or glimpse God's transformative work happening through you to bring about eternal change. Vision is really about allowing God to direct us toward new ideas, new ways of doing things, and new places of ministry that we haven't thought of before.

I'm not suggesting that you can't have a calling if you're not an optimistic or creative type of person. This isn't about personality. But the articulation of a calling should take the form of a preferred future that you are actively pursuing and that captures the imagination of others.

There's a Japanese proverb that says, "Vision without action is a daydream and action with without vision is a nightmare." In other words, your calling needs an aim, and taking action toward that aim is how you will fulfill your calling. The writer of Proverbs says it this way:

Where there is no vision, the people perish.

Proverbs 29:18, KJV

A clear vision provides a picture of a brighter future and a hopeful view of what God is doing. Ultimately, we are moving toward the glorious future of Christ reigning over all things and making all things new. As we wait for that final destination, God "… is able to do immeasurably more than all we ask or imagine" (Ephesians 3:20, NIV). God's ways are always higher than ours, and vision helps us tap into what he is doing in the world. Vision, propelled by faith that God is bringing all nations to himself, has the power to inspire both ourselves and those who will come alongside us to carry out our calling.

PASSION

The immediate sidekick to vision is passion. Passion is an intense desire or enthusiasm for something. It's an inner motivation that leads to outward action. I know I'm passionate about something when I am eager to do it. For example, I rarely need motivation to run because it's become a life passion for me. You may have heard people say that if you're passionate about your vocation, you'll never work a day in your life. Although work may be difficult at times, if you're passionate about it and that passion points to a calling, you will make it through the ups and downs.

Every compelling vision inspires passion. As you consider your calling to serve in cross-cultural ministry and the words of Jesus in the Great Commission, are you not propelled into action? Just as a coach's pregame pep talk will not propel the team into action if it lacks passion, so also your calling, if it is not backed up with passion, will not inspire others to come alongside and join you in the work.

The problem is, you cannot produce a burning passion for the vision of your calling by yourself. This is a work of the Spirit of God. Your part in the process is to pursue a deeper relationship with God daily and ask him to give you his passion for the calling he has given you.

The apostle Paul is a prime example of a man with deep passion for the spread of the gospel. Imagine you are listening to Paul—the one who was shipwrecked, snake bitten, beaten nearly to death, imprisoned, and persecuted—utter these words:

> *"I make it my ambition to preach the gospel."*

Romans 15:20

> *"... for me to live is Christ, and to die is gain."*

Philippians 1:21

> "How then will they call on him in whom they have not believed? And how are they to believe in him of whom they have never heard? And how are they to hear without someone preaching? And how are they to preach unless they are sent? As it is written, 'How beautiful are the feet of those who preach the good news!'"

Romans 10:14, 15

Now that is the kind of passion that can inspire a whole movement!

When God called me to the ministry of missions mobilization, my passion for the work had to catch up with my prayer and vision. The mobilizer I would eventually replace asked me to pray about taking on his job when he moved on. The first time he mentioned it, I instantly said no, but I did commit to pray about it. I clearly had no vision for the ministry at that point, but as I prayed, God began helping me see the possibilities.

On the second occasion my friend mentioned me for this role, I had enough growing interest to ask questions. I had been asking my close friends and mentors to advise me and pray with me about the opportunity. But without passion for missions mobilization, I still wasn't ready to articulate it as a calling or even move toward it.

Encompass waited patiently as I asked the Lord for direction—and it came in his good timing. I eventually found myself at a missions leadership gathering focused on raising up the next generation for global missions, and while I was there I realized that I shared the passion of many other leaders in the room who longed to see the next generation take their place in global missions. My prayers for direction were answered, and I came away from that event with both vision and passion to see my peers and future generations making disciples of the nations.

The combination of prayer, vision, and passion worked together to not only confirm my calling, but also sustain me through the past ten years as Director of Missions Mobilization at Encompass. It's been a tremendous joy to watch others embark on the same journey and discover a calling that was unique to them and designed by God.

It's a journey that requires faith in a big God.

At Encompass, one of our core values is, "Prayer that leads to vision, that leads to risk-taking faith." The risk of faith is in good hands when we seek God in prayer and ask him to lead us. The journey to discern your calling requires faith that God will answer your prayers, give you a vision for the future, and place a passion in your heart to live out that calling for his glory.

 DIGGING DEEPER

Questions to Consider

1. What role has prayer played in your journey to discern God's call? In light of what you read in this chapter, are there new or different ways you want to pray about it?

2. How can you invite others to pray for you as you consider your next steps? What people is God laying on your heart as possible prayer partners?

3. How is God developing in you a vision for future ministry? What does it look like?

4. Would your friends describe you as passionate about the vision God is giving you?

5. How could your passions help you move toward the vision God has given you?

Scriptures to Consider

↓ *Psalm 96:3, 4; Proverbs 3:1–8; Daniel 9:1–9; Luke 10:2; Romans 10:14–17*

CALLED: WE SHOULD MOVE HERE

Being full-time global workers was never on the radar for Kevin and Jill.

But God had other plans. Kevin and Jill met Christ later in life, and they became involved with Wooster Grace Church in Ohio. Living out their newfound faith, they joined several ministry teams and served their neighbors and others in the community. A few years later, during one of the church's Missions Emphasis Weeks, Kevin and Jill attended a ministry presentation about the spiritual needs of Cambodia.

At the time, Jill was going through a Bible study in Genesis and had just read about the call of Abraham. With that story fresh in her mind, Jill listened to Cambodia's need for Jesus and felt clearly drawn to minister there. In her heart, she said to God, "Here I am, Lord. Send me." The experience closely resembled the day she first met Jesus.

Kevin felt very differently, though.

After the presentation, he asked Jill what she thought, and she said simply, "I want to go." She meant that she wanted to go to Cambodia long-term, but Kevin assumed she was talking about the short-term missions trip the church was planning. He was shocked and a little disapproving. He loved her heart, but there was no way they were going to Cambodia.

Jill said nothing more and prayed for God's will to be done.

In the weeks following, Cambodia began to pop up everywhere. It was in the news, on the National Geographic Channel, and mentioned in random conversations. Jill's call began to feel more like a burden than a joy. Knowing that God would not split them on an issue like this, Jill continued to pray for her husband's heart to be opened.

God answered her prayer one little step at a time.

First, Kevin came home from work one afternoon to eat lunch while Jill was studying Genesis. That day's lesson was about Abraham lying to King Abimelech, telling him that Sarah was his sister. As Kevin sat down at the table, Jill asked him, "Do you think Abraham was trusting in God when he lied about Sarah, or was he using his own common sense?"

Kevin quickly responded, "Of course he wasn't trusting in God; that's a no-brainer."

After lunch, Kevin went back to the house he was working on renovating. As he drove, his wife's question lingered in his heart. He had felt the Lord prodding him to go to Cambodia before this, but he had refused to acknowledge it. He thought anyone with an ounce of common sense would not go to Cambodia in the midst of their political instability. Fear was getting in his way, and in his heart, Kevin knew he was not trusting in God.

Back at work, Kevin's task that afternoon was to paint a closet, and as he worked, he prayed over his fear. The two requests he had for the Lord were stretch me and break me. Kevin met with God for hours, wrestling with him like never before. He emerged from the closet drenched with sweat and drove straight home. He walked into the kitchen and told Jill, "We're going!"

Six months later, they were on a plane to Cambodia for a short-term missions trip. Near the end of the first day of the trip, Kevin said, "You know, Jill, you should really come back here on the next short-term missions trip." It was a start.

The next day, after several hours of serving and exploring, Kevin turned to his wife and said, "You know, Jill, we should both come back here on the next short-term missions trip."

On the fifth day, Kevin looked at Jill and said, "I think God wants us to move here."

With great joy, Jill explained how she had felt the Lord's call from the very beginning to serve in Cambodia long-term.

Kevin and Jill have faithfully spread the gospel in Cambodia for 12 years. In those early days, both Kevin and Jill faced a choice: to obey God, trusting even when it didn't make sense, or to push for their own agenda. The joy they found in choosing obedient faith is a shining example of the truth of the old hymn:

> *Then in fellowship sweet, we will sit at His feet,*
> *Or we'll walk by His side in the way;*
> *What He says we will do; where He sends we will go;*
> *Never fear, only trust and obey.*

CHAPTER 3
FACING THE BARRIERS

This week, my two oldest sons start a new soccer season. The excitement has been building, and their love for the game and the enjoyment of playing with their friends grows with each season. Unfortunately, a recent playground injury has left our ten-year-old hobbled with a bone bruise. Watching my kids endure pain is one of the hardest things about parenting, and the timing of this injury has been particularly hard on our son, who just wants to get out there and play. His heart wills him to play, but instead he must sit out and recover from his injury. In other words, he has encountered a barrier—one he must face with courage and faith.

BARRIERS ARE INEVITABLE. JESUS TOLD US THAT FOLLOWING HIM WILL COME WITH ADVERSITY.

> *Whoever wants to be my disciple must deny themselves and take up their cross daily and follow me.*
>
> **Luke 9:23, NIV**

Pursuing a calling comes with a fair amount of opposition. Missions is spiritual warfare, and as we take steps that may lead us into the thick of the spiritual battle, we must be aware that we have an adversary who wants to stop us before we even take our first steps. Because of this, it's not a question of *if* but a question of *when* you'll face barriers. Facing these barriers has the ability to refine your character, expand your faith, and help confirm your calling. But in order to reap these positive benefits, you need to be prepared to courageously face barriers and overcome. This is why we want to spend some time considering some of the barriers you will face as you prayerfully discern God's leading.

I am an avid mountain biker, and I enjoy introducing others to the thrill of the sport. But I would never take a beginner on the expert black diamond trials without warning him of the obstacles that lie ahead. I wouldn't be a very good guide, and my beginner friend, if not injured, would at least be questioning whether he could trust me. As we embark on the journey of discerning God's call to serve in cross-cultural ministry, I want to be a good guide who points out some of the common obstacles or barriers that have been faced by those who have gone before: finances, family, and fear.

FINANCES

As you consider full-time, cross-cultural ministry, you probably have questions about personal finances, the challenges of debt, and raising financial support or what we call ministry partner development. Related to each of these are misconceptions about financial livelihood and sustainability. Let's work through these one at a time.

1. **The Challenges of Debt**—It is rare to find missions-interested people who don't have some kind of financial debt to overcome. It could be a car payment, a mortgage, an outstanding credit card, student loans, or some combination of these. It is likely that you have more than one form of debt, and the total may be daunting as you think of moving overseas.

   The Bible speaks to the issues of debt, and we all agree that being debt-free is the preferred position for those considering future ministry, but having debt is a barrier that can be overcome. If you are one of the few who haven't taken on debt, it is wise to do all you can to avoid it in an effort to be more available to respond to God's call.

The soaring amount of student loans among young people who are praying and dreaming about serving as missionaries has caused some missions sending agencies to create policies to help those who have a manageable level of qualified student debt. Each agency has its own set of values and criteria for how they approach debt before going and while on the field. We believe that the personal burden of debt and the decisions that surround it should be discussed and agreed upon with the leadership of your church, as they serve an important role in sending. Just because an agency has a policy in place doesn't mean all who are eligible should use it—trust your convictions and consult with your sending church.

If you are in debt, large or small, I highly encourage you to prayerfully and aggressively focus on paying it off. You're investing in future ministry. Adjusting to life in another country is challenging enough without adding the financial and mental burden of debt. Also, living within a budget and paying off debt will help you develop healthy stewardship muscles that will serve you well when you're managing donor funds and your ministry budget. Finally, let me note that the kind of guidance mentioned here is not professional financial advice. You may benefit from seeking the help of a professional to write your roadmap to becoming debt-free. In addition, there are many Christian books and websites dedicated to helping people pay off debt, and those can be helpful as you get a handle on your financial situation.

2. **Ministry Partner Development**—This is commonly known as support-raising, and it is the number one objection for many people who are considering missions. Some people search for other options to fund their ministry, but gathering financial partners is still the way that the majority of full-time ministry workers fund and sustain ministry.

We don't have time to do a comprehensive Bible study on the topic here, but throughout the Scriptures, God uses his people to provide for the work of the gospel. There are countless examples, particularly in the ministry of Paul, of churches sending out missionaries and providing for their needs and their work. This model brings encouragement and joy to both the giver and the receiver. In addition, it helps sending churches be more invested in prayer support as well. If our heart is where our treasure is, then it stands to reason that if we send our treasure to workers in another country, our heart and our prayers will follow.

The process of finding ministry partners who will contribute to your financial needs is one of the ways God will grow your faith. For perhaps the first time in your adult life, your financial needs are out of your control. You have to pray and wait for God to provide. And when he does, you will be encouraged by the answer to prayer and bolstered by others' confidence in your call.

The faith of your ministry partners will also grow through their role on your team. They have to seek the Lord's will for their finances and trust him to provide for their needs as well as their giving. Later on, as you share what God is doing to make his name known among the nations, they will be encouraged and get excited to fulfill their role in the Great Commission as well. You can become a catalyst to mobilize individuals and churches to be active in God's work by inviting them to partner with you. Missions leader Tom Julien often says it this way: "Missions is not what the church does for the missionary, but through the missionary."

3. **Misconceptions to Address**—Some people who are interested in cross-cultural missions believe that going into missions means they must take a vow of poverty, and for them this becomes a barrier to following God's call. God leads some people to live in poverty with the people they serve, but that's not true of most missionaries. We shouldn't expect to be impoverished, because there are many resources available to fund missions. In fact, healthy and sustainable finances are an advantage to missions work because they allow workers to stay focused on the mission and not be distracted by their bills. This is why most agencies create fundraising goals that include salary, benefits, and all the expenses associated with your ministry, both in the preparation beforehand and for the duration of your time on the field. Add to that cost of living adjustments based on where you are going to serve in the world, and you have a pretty

comprehensive financial package that will help you get onto the field and stay there.

The mission of God cannot advance with a scarcity mind-set. Pioneer missionary to China Hudson Taylor famously said, "God's work, done God's way, will never lack God's supply." God can use the challenges of funding ministry to teach us, prepare us, and affirm his calling for us as we put our faith in him.

FAMILY

Whether you're single or married with children, family considerations are a big part of the discernment journey. Perhaps you have the responsibility of caring for a family member in need, or your family just doesn't support you moving so far away. If you have children, you could be weighed down by how they will be impacted by your decision to live cross-culturally. Whatever your circumstances, the expectations, responsibilities, and limitations of your family are major factors to prayerfully consider as you take next steps.

I had the opportunity to talk about discerning God's call to missions at a conference a few years ago, and I'll never forget a young lady who asked me, "What do you do when your parents are in complete opposition to you going into missions?" The way she asked the question revealed how disappointed she was with her parents, who I learned later had asked that she not even talk about it anymore.

On the other hand, I had the opportunity to be present for the commissioning of a good friend whose family was preparing to go to Africa. I sat next to my friend's mother, who had recently become a widow. Most wouldn't blame her for not wanting to release her kids and grandkids, but when I approached her after the service to share words of encouragement, her response amazed me. She said that she knew this was what God had planned for her son, and it was her joy to watch him do it.

Family circumstances can vary, but I'm convinced that the biggest barriers to overcome are the unfilled expectations of family who long to be close relationally and assume that will necessitate being close geographically. One of the best things you can do is to bring family along with you on your journey of discernment. Help them see the need and opportunity, and ask them to pray with you about it. This approach is better than telling them after you've made the decision and expecting them to support you with very little input. If your family isn't following Jesus this can be especially hard, but it could also be the means God uses to do an amazing work in your family.

If you are married and your spouse isn't supportive, I recommend that you not move ahead until you are on the same page. The only thing that will change your spouse's heart is the Holy Spirit, so pray that he will. Unlike other vocational callings, a call to missions really needs to be a shared vision for both the husband and the wife. The important thing here is honest communication and praying for God's leading in your lives as a couple. When spouses go along with the consideration for missions because they don't want to disappoint or discourage their partner, it is always disastrous and difficult to recover from. However, when both husband and wife have had their own sense of God's leading, it's a great affirmation for how God can use you together in missions.

Jesus spoke pretty directly to his disciples, and while this may be more descriptive than prescriptive for us today, it still resonates.

> *Everyone who has left houses or brothers or sisters or father or mother or children or lands, for my name's sake, will receive a hundredfold and will inherit eternal life.*

Matthew 19:29

As your family follows Jesus, you have an eternal inheritance to look forward to. But until then there's work to be done, and the cause of Christ might mean temporal sacrifice not just for the ones who go, but also for those who are left behind.

FEAR

The final barrier we'll address is fear. Fear can take many forms when you consider serving as a missionary. We've just talked about the fear of separation from family, and before that we delved into the fear of financial uncertainty. Those can be the cause of deep anxiety, but one of the biggest barriers you'll face is fear for your own safety.

Psychologists tell us that decision making most often centers around the primary feelings of pleasure and pain. In other words, what motivates our decisions is our desire for pleasure and our desire not to feel pain. It is not so with the gospel. We stand on the truth of the gospel today because of the saints who have gone before us, who gave up earthly pleasures and endured pain even unto death so that the cause of Christ would persist and advance to those who are living without hope. This is what Jesus did for us on the cross, and we are called to do the same, dying to ourselves so that we can lay down our lives for our brothers and sisters. Jesus said it this way in the gospel of John:

> *Truly, truly, I say to you, unless a grain of wheat falls into the earth and dies, it remains alone; but if it dies, it bears much fruit.*

John 12:24

As Jesus prepared to send out his disciples for the first time in Matthew 10, he warned that they would be flogged, arrested, hated, persecuted, and even killed. He was pretty up front about the barriers his disciples would face. But he was also clear about the rewards that awaited them and those who received their message, saying, "whoever loses his life for my sake will find it" (Matthew 10:39).

The mission of the church has been hindered by the "safety first" mind-set that is prevalent in our North American culture today. God's saving grace promises eternal security, but according to Jesus, the call to make disciples of all nations puts us at risk of earthly harm. The mission of God cannot advance with a safety mind-set.

When you get right down to it, all of our fears (including finances, family, and safety) are wrapped up in the fear of the unknown. Leaving a familiar place, culture, language, customs, and systems to choose the unknown soil of a new … well, everything … comes with a high degree of uncertainty. When we fill in the unknown with anxious thoughts about what might happen and live as if those scary things are all going to happen, we become riddled with fear.

I recently heard this acronym for FEAR: False Expectations Appearing Real. I'll admit sometimes these pithy statements can come off as cliché, like the church sign I read this week that said, "God answers knee-mail." But this one got me thinking because most of my fears of the unknown come from false expectations that are not based in reality.

The spiritual battles we engage in with our adversary, Satan, are in and for the mind. Satan wants to paralyze us with fear, and as long as he can keep us believing lies, we won't act on the truths that Jesus wants us to embrace. In the same passage we looked at earlier in Matthew 10, where Jesus issues warnings to his disciples, he also says multiple times to not be afraid or worried.

In our house we quote Joshua 1:9 all the time. In fact, we gave our third son the middle name Joshua because this verse has become a theme verse for our family.

Be strong and courageous. Do not be frightened, and do not be dismayed, for the Lord your God is with you wherever you go.

Joshua 1:9

Faith in God's promises is the only way forward as you face barriers in the journey to discern your calling. Indeed, lack of faith in God and the truth of his promises is the biggest barrier of them all. Don't get me wrong—God can still use people like Zechariah, who doubted his plans as we read in Luke 1. But Zechariah's story appears next to Mary's for a reason. They both played an important part in God's plan of redemption, but Mary's response to the angel Gabriel is one of faith and trust, and she is honored for it.

"I am the Lord's servant," Mary answered. "May your word to me be fulfilled."

Luke 1:38, NIV

It shouldn't surprise us that the Bible speaks with authoritative truth to the barriers of finances, family, and fear. As you seek answers to some of the barriers we've talked about, you might discover that the opportunity to go and serve as a missionary isn't the best path forward at this time. God may be revealing things that you need to work through in faith before you take the next step. That doesn't mean your calling is being undermined, but it's comforting to know that facing the barriers can be part of God's preparation to help you grow in faith.

 ## DIGGING DEEPER

Questions to Consider

1. What are your top five barriers to cross-cultural ministry?

2. How does each one hold you back?

3. Spend time praying through each of these barriers, asking God to speak into them. What is he telling you?

4. What are some specific next steps you can take to overcome these barriers?

Scriptures to Consider

> *2 Chronicles 20:1–34; Acts 20:24; Ephesians 3:14–20; Philippians 3:12–14; 2 Timothy 1:6–9*

CALLED: EVERYTHING CHANGED IN LINCOLN

As a high school student in St. Louis, Dan felt a tug toward global ministry. He wanted to dive in after graduation, and several opportunities presented themselves. Dan's pastor told him about an outdoor adventure ministry in Japan called NORTHSTAR, and at the same time an outreach ministry in Bosnia came to his attention. Dan decided to pursue moving to Bosnia, but

God had a different path in mind. The plan for Bosnia fell apart, and Dan had to put his desire to move overseas on hold.

Instead, Dan went to Missouri State University to study criminology, and while he was there, he met April.

April hadn't even considered global ministry. She was a track star at Missouri State, majoring in Recreational Studies. She planned to become a personal trainer and break into the health industry. She and Dan began dating, and when April made the decision to return to her home state of Oklahoma to finish school, they continued their relationship even though they were far apart. After graduation, they got married.

Going straight from a long-distance relationship to marriage was hard. Their first year brought to light many issues that they hadn't been aware of, and things got rough enough that they considered divorce. Instead, Dan and April made the decision to fight for their marriage. They decided to get a fresh start by moving to a new city and starting over.

They moved to Lincoln, Nebraska.

A pastor from a local church let Dan and April live in his basement, and they were able to see the pastor and his wife model what a Christ-centered marriage looks like. Through their influence, Dan and April grew in their love for God and each other, and their marriage began to revive.

After six months, Dan and April moved out of the basement and joined a house church called Jacob's Well, which ministered to needy families in downtown Lincoln. They helped host block parties, gave food away to neighbors, and occasionally helped with after-school programs for the kids. A passion for cross-cultural ministry began to grow in their hearts. For Dan it was a return to his roots, and for April it was a new desire, but now it was a vision they shared. After four years in Lincoln, they asked God what he might have for them next.

That's when Dan heard about NORTHSTAR for the second time.

A friend brought up the Japanese outdoor ministry, and it was a great fit for Dan and April. They went to Japan for short-term service with NORTHSTAR, and their time there kindled a love for the Japanese people. Back home, Dan and April talked about long-term ministry in Japan.

The only thing still holding them back was their desire to start a family. They thought they had to make a choice between having children and moving overseas. They wrestled with the decision for a while before coming to see that God might want them to pursue both. They had already experienced how shared ministry could strengthen their family. They began to take steps toward becoming full-time global workers just as they discovered that they were pregnant.

Dan and April are new parents to their son Lincoln, named after the city in Nebraska where they took their first steps toward restoring their relationship and finding their common mission. They are excited to return to Japan as a family and see what God has for them there together.

CHAPTER 4
CULTIVATING YOUR COMMUNITY

GOD MAKES IT VERY CLEAR THROUGHOUT HIS WORD: HUMANS AREN'T MEANT TO LIVE IN ISOLATION.

This is especially true in ministry. You need a community to surround you with prayer, friendship, accountability, mentorship, and guidance. It's hard for me to imagine what my life would look like if I didn't have a solid community of people who are also committed to following Jesus encouraging me and walking with me. A church like the one that Paul's writes to in Thessalonica, where he commends them for being a community of people committed to Christ and each other.

> We cared so much for you that we were pleased to share with
> you not only the gospel of God but also our own lives, because
> you had become dear to us.

1 Thessalonians 2:8, HCSB

Paul and his missionary comrades had been sent out by the church in Antioch, and it was their goal to see the gospel spread by showing God's love and sharing their lives with others. In the next chapter, we'll talk more about the relationship or partnership of the church, the agency, and the missionary to sustain the work of missions. In this chapter, we want to focus on cultivating a community of friends, family, and spiritual mentors who can encourage you and can also be truth tellers for you as you discern your calling.

Before Paul shared the words above he said in chapter one,

> *You know how we lived among you for your sake. You became imitators*
> *of us and of the Lord.... And so you became a model to all the believers in*
> *Macedonia and Achaia.*

1 Thessalonians 1:5–7, NIV

We all need that kind of community, people who will model lives of faithfully following Jesus and spur us on to do the same. If you have this already, now is the time to lean into them for answers to the big questions you are pondering and ask them to advise you and pray for you. If you don't have this kind of community, it's time to start seeking it out and asking God to surround you with people you can share your life with.

Many lone rangers who have gone out to serve as missionaries have left a wake of brokenness behind them. We are not meant to go alone, because the lessons we must learn about being a disciple of Jesus and making disciples of Jesus are best learned in community. Close friends can speak into your growth in Christ and encourage you to have healthy habits and practices that will mature your faith and create ripple effects into your future ministry. The patterns of discipleship that you learn from Christian community in your home culture will enable you to establish healthy communities in the places you serve.

I'll never forget approaching my mentor of then six years about the consideration I was giving to a future ministry opportunity, only to have him say without hesitation, "Of course that would be a great ministry fit for your gifts and abilities!" From there I expanded the community of people I talked with and trusted to advise me and pray with me, and I just kept hearing the same thing. Remember, our definition of calling includes "confirmed by the body of Christ." Your community helps you discern your calling. And it's these people who will tell you the truth if they don't sense you are ready to step into cross-cultural ministry. Who else will be honest with you, if not your close friends?

It's a beautiful thing to watch Christian community respond to the movement of God in someone's life. I work with another missions mobilizer who is preparing to go and serve overseas. She's currently living and serving with Encompass at a distance from where she grew up. She recently traveled back home to grow her team of prayer and financial partners, and she was overwhelmed by the hospitality and generosity of the community that she had cultivated back home despite the years that had passed. I was happy that she experienced this, but I wasn't surprised. I know how she lives and shares her life with others. In situations like hers, the body of Christ should respond with loving support and affirmation of calling. The metaphor of the body implies that each part supports the other, and it gives us joy to share our lives and serve one another.

As I was writing this chapter, I was reminded of how Paul often honored his brothers and sisters who were also doing the work of the gospel in their areas. He was not alone, but worked in partnership with his sending community. Consider his request for prayer to the Colossians.

> *Continue steadfastly in prayer, being watchful in it with thanksgiving. At the same time, pray also for us, that God may open to us a door for the word, to declare the mystery of Christ, on account of which I am in prison—that I may make it clear, which is how I ought to speak.*

Colossians 4:2–4

Immediately after this prayer request for open doors and clear speaking, Paul rattles off the names of ten faithful partners who were sharing in the work of proclaiming Christ throughout the region. His ministry was not his own; it was shared.

I know without a doubt that I couldn't do the ministry God has called me to do without the community that is faithfully partnering with me. The old proverb says "it takes a village," but in this case, it takes the body of Christ to raise up, send, and support the work of those who will serve as cross-cultural workers. You can't underestimate the importance of cultivating your community, and should God call you as a missionary, you should be able to look back, like Paul did with the Colossians, and share with joy what God is doing through you together.

 DIGGING DEEPER

Questions to Consider

1. Dream and pray about what it might look like to have a community of support behind you while you serve in cross-cultural ministry: friends, family, brothers and sisters in Christ, and spiritual mentors. How do you envision that support network forming?

2. How will it impact your life and ministry to have this support network? How could it impact those who partner with you?

3. Who are you already bringing along with you on this journey toward cross-cultural ministry? Do they have permission to speak even difficult truths into your life as you discern your next steps?

4. Who else in your community could you share with as you expand your network and draw closer to the day when it will be time to ask for specific help in going—prayer warriors and financial donors?

5. What do you need to do next to cultivate your community?

Scriptures to Consider

Acts 2:42–47; Philippians 1:3, 4; Colossians 3:12–17

CALLED: JOURNEY TO GERMANY

On family road trips, did your parents tell you that the joy is as much in the journey as the destination? Usually this statement followed an expression of impatience from you or a sibling who wished teleportation was possible. Of course "the journey is half the fun" talk left little remedy for your back-seat sorrow. The truth is that when God takes you from point A to point B, every little step is a blessing that enriches the destination.

Jo's journey is a perfect example of this.

As a high school senior, Jo had no idea what she wanted to do with her life. Her church was not globally minded, so missions was not on her radar as she looked for career options. Unable to find direction before her senior year concluded, she attended a community college, hoping to figure things out there. As a student, she started working with Fellowship of Christian Athletes, a ministry that focuses on reaching youth through sports. Jo loved playing basketball and quickly found that using her athletic talents for ministry was something she enjoyed. She began to wonder if ministry was the path God was calling her to. She decided to pursue Biblical training from Grace College in Winona Lake, Indiana, to gain valuable preparation.

While at Grace, Jo's major required her to spend one semester abroad, so she began contacting missions sending agencies to find one that would partner with her in her time overseas. She was drawn to Encompass World Partners because she wanted to work with an agency that would come around her as part of her team. Jo discovered there is great need for the gospel in places like Europe, so she geared up to spend her semester abroad in Germany using basketball as a platform for ministry. While there, she felt a distinct call to commit her life to missions.

After returning to the States, all Jo could think about was going back.

She wanted to get approved for ministry, raise support, and be deployed as quickly as possible. She knew, however, the importance of having a sending church and wanted Winona Lake Grace Brethren Church to send her. This meant a two-year period of training before she could get back to Germany. Her mobilizer at Encompass encouraged her to embrace the time of transition, and use it to effectively educate her supporters on what she wanted to do, as well as plant seeds among her unbelieving friends.

During this two-year waiting period, Jo took a short-term trip to Germany to help refugees who had fled there. The trip to Germany helped Jo sharpen her ministry focus and gave her a desire to help the churches there minister to refugees—an opportunity she would have missed had she taken the "fast track."

Jo's story is an example of how God is working even in the "down time." God will bring exactly what you need when you need it, including direction. Every step is as important as the destination, and being missional even on the way to missions is a blessing. You may be at the front of your journey to missions, right in the middle, or so close you can see the end. You might not even be on the journey, but wondering if you should be. Wherever you are, it's important to know that God is at work every step of the way. Always seek the Lord in prayer and be missional where you are right now.

CHAPTER 5

THE ESSENTIAL ROLE OF A SENDING CHURCH

THE JOY OF HEARING GOD'S CALL TO MISSIONS IS UNLIKE ANYTHING ELSE.

When we feel the power of Christ's commission to go and make disciples of all nations and see a vision of what can be accomplished, we are ready to do it. We are eager and inspired, excited to share the hope of Jesus with a world in need.

But from the moment we step onto the field in a new place, we face internal and external pressures we didn't expect. Cultural and language barriers make us feel out of place. We find ourselves watched and judged from new angles. People don't respond to our message in ways we expect. We grow tired. Things that start out as small challenges grow and threaten to break up our teams and families.

Within a year or two, many new missionaries who start with great vision and passion are ready to pack their bags and fly home.

The good news is that Jesus didn't just tell us to do a job and leave us alone to do it. He gave us his Spirit to lead and guide us, and his body, the Church, to prepare us, release us, and help us navigate difficult seasons. The burnout that so often happens in a missionary's first few years can be avoided by tapping into these resources God has provided. This is why the role of the sending church is essential to being prepared, sent, and sustained in cross-cultural ministry.

Remember the definition of calling...

> *"God's call is an inner conviction given by and through the Holy Spirit and confirmed by the Word of God, the body of Christ, and the character of the called."*
>
> **Ryan Johnston**[7]

We can observe a pattern that started at the church in Antioch in the book of Acts, and is an example for us today as we seek to obey Jesus' command to go and make disciple of all nations.

THE CHURCH IN ANTIOCH

In Acts 13, the church in Antioch was worshiping God, seeking him in prayer, and fasting. It was at this moment, in the context of worship, that they were called as workers, and it was a call from the Holy Spirit. He was the one who "sent" Paul and Barnabas, and it was only after that commissioning that they were "released" by the local church for their mission (v. 2, 3).

Throughout the rest of the book of Acts, the mission team made decisions on the field under the instruction of the Holy Spirit. He was a constant, guiding presence, and it was because of this supernatural helper that Paul was able to live with such great apostolic focus and strategy. He mobilized others from local churches, raising up disciples and equipping them for the work under the power and presence of the Holy Spirit.

If we want to have a ministry that is both powerful and persevering, we must rely on the help of the Holy Spirit. However, let's not forget the Holy Spirit spoke not just to Paul and Barnabas, but also to the leaders of the church in Antioch. Too often we can get excited about the prompting of the Holy Spirit in our own lives without seeking the counsel of leaders in the church or others in

[7] Ryan Johnston. *Examining the "Call" to Ministry* (theHSF.com: 2011)

the body of Christ which God has given to affirm and confirm his leading.

Let's continue by looking at why this example from the Bible is essential for the church today.

THE SENDING CHURCH TODAY

Missionaries are sent, sustained, and shepherded by the local sending church. A close look at Scripture and more than a century of work in the world's least-reached places have taught us that mobilizing and sustaining missionaries works best in relationship with a sending church or home church. In the early church, mission teams maintained a deep, partnering connection with their home church. They returned for visits, wrote letters, prayed together, shared mutual encouragement, and gave thanks for their partnership in the gospel.

The relationship between the church and missions work in the New Testament went both ways. Churches sent short-term workers, finances, supplies, and prayer. We see Paul constantly growing his relationship with churches and relying on them for support. And this wasn't mere lip service—he truly needed them. Indeed, in Philippians 1:3–7, Paul calls the believers in Philippi his partners in ministry.

The relationship between a missionary and a sending church makes the gospel come to life locally and globally. From identifying the right laborers, to sustaining the work, to engaging more disciple-makers, the relationship between missionaries and churches drives the mission. A sending church partners with its missionaries to provide spiritual, pastoral, and sometimes financial support. And missionaries provide sending churches with opportunities to extend their reach and to experience and learn from God's work around the world.

The sending church also confirms a missionary's call and gives authenticity to their message. If we want to know a person's growth and obedience to Christ, we ask how that person has walked in obedience to Christ within the community of the local church. A missionary known for integrity in her home church will be known for integrity in the field. A missionary prone to conflict at his home church will carry that tendency into the field.

Recently a missionary family suffered from a dangerous situation on the field. The situation rattled them and made them question the work to which they were called. The sending agency reached out to their home church to prepare for an evacuation. When they returned home, the hurting family was met with a caring community that was ready to walk with them through the healing process. The home church even provided for their practical needs, finding housing and a vehicle for them. This is a great example of how local churches provide the spiritual and relational care that missionaries need.

These opportunities to provide care bring local churches to life. Many missionaries are now on the field because they joined a short-term team through their local church. Others back home are inspired to greater discipleship by hearing the stories of missionaries who share how God is working in and through them.

A COMMISSION ENTRUSTED TO THE CHURCH

I recently had the joy of watching a local church commission a family for work overseas. The pastor, elders, missions team, and some close friends gathered around to shower them with love, prayers, and affirmation in their mission. After walking with this family through the whole process of mobilization, seeing them released to their mission with so much love was a profound experience. This is the local church and the missionary working under the direction of the Spirit of God! The discipleship the church had invested, their words of affirmation, their prayers, and their ongoing care will be a sustaining force in the life of this family in the years to come. And this family's work will, in turn, bless, excite, and deepen the life of the church in their pursuit of God's mission.

Missionaries are the feet, hands, and voice of Jesus, offering a bold and consistent witness of who God is and what he has accomplished through Christ. They sow the essence and the glory of the Church to be reproduced in any given culture. To do all this work sustainably and in close relationship with Christ, every missionary needs to understand that when God calls us to go, he doesn't call us to go alone.

The gospel exploded throughout the world by the work of missionaries sent by local churches and led with apostolic authority from the New Testament. Those biblical models hold just as true today.

Under the spiritual guidance of the Holy Spirit, together with the essential role of a sending church, missionaries will be equipped to live and make disciples among new peoples, until every tribe and tongue confesses that Jesus Christ is Lord.

 DIGGING DEEPER

Questions to Consider

1. Does your church have a global ministry emphasis? If so, what is that emphasis and how could you become a part of it?

2. Are there intentional steps your church has established to prepare missionaries? What are they?

3. What do the leaders of your church ask you to do to prepare for missions and be sent by the church?

4. What people or resources should you connect with as you consider your next steps? Ask the leaders of your church.

Scriptures to Consider

Matthew 28:17–20; Acts 1:8; 13:1–3; I Peter 4:10, 11

Saul and Carol started out on similar paths.

They were both born in Southern California, grew up in Christian families, and attended the same college. However, the vision each of them had for their future vocation was quite different.

From the time she was a little girl, Carol always wanted to work in international ministry. She heard the inspiring stories of visiting missionaries and was determined to one day serve abroad. This passion matured and went along with her all the way to college.

On the other hand, Saul was not sure what he wanted to do. He became a Christian at a young age, but he did not ever consider missions as a possibility. However, by the time he got to college, Saul's one great passion was to do what God wanted him to do. This was a great attitude to have when he met his future wife, Carol.

Saul and Carol started dating in college. As they explored their relationship, they also explored the possibility of a future in global missions. They began attending a church in Simi Valley, where they discovered Encompass World Partners, and through them Saul got connected to an internship in Central Asia.

Saul had a wonderful experience working alongside Encompass workers Mickey and Shelly Bernard in Central Asia. After returning to the States, he was excited about serving in missions like never before. His internship was exactly the kind of exposure he needed.

Saul and Carol got married, and the big question on the table was *should we go into missions immediately after graduation?*

They asked their family, friends, and church community for advice. The responses varied. Some people told them to go right away, others advised waiting for little while before going, and some people told them not to go at all.

In the end, Saul and Carol decided that waiting was the best option.

For the next five years, they built up their marriage, friends, and skill sets. They became heavily involved with their local church and pursued further education, all the while prayerfully discerning their vision for missions.

One of the most valuable experiences they had during this time was visiting the Bernard family, Saul's hosts in Central Asia. Mickey and Shelly were transitioning from their ministry in Central Asia to Southeast Asia. During this transition, they lived in Long Beach, California, for one year and periodically visited Saul and Carol's church. Knowing the two had interest in serving cross-culturally, the Bernards were very intentional in reaching out to them.

Eventually, the Bernards asked Saul and Carol if they wanted to join their team in Southeast Asia. Up to this point they had never thought much about where they wanted to go. Instead, they thought more about who they wanted to go with, and they had been in contact with Encompass as they considered next steps.

After a great deal of prayer and counsel, Saul and Carol decided to take the Bernards up on their offer. They flew to the Bernards' new home in Southeast Asia for an exploratory trip, and their calling was confirmed. The defining factor in their decision was how much they loved the Bernards and their team.

Because Saul and Carol waited and continued to prayerfully move toward the goal of serving as missionaries, they were well prepared for their new calling. They were able to raise support quickly, they had gained masters-level education that helped them find a needed job opportunity, and their marriage was stronger than ever. Plus, they found the right teammates to serve with.

Choosing the right team is crucial, and should be done prayerfully and patiently.

CHAPTER 6

PARTNERING WITH A SENDING AGENCY

YOU'VE DISCERNED THAT GOD IS CALLING YOU TO MISSIONS, AND IT'S TAKEN A LOT OF THOUGHT AND PRAYER TO GET TO THIS POINT.

Perhaps you're excited and can't wait to get on the field—or perhaps the discernment journey has been exhausting, and you need a little time to recuperate before you take the next step.

The truth is, the journey is far from over. In fact, in many ways it's just beginning. I think this is why we see the Apostle Paul talking often about the need for patient endurance. There are still so many unknowns: Where will you go? When? What will you do? How will you get there? With all these questions swirling in your mind, you may end up with option fatigue. The innumerable variables to consider can become overwhelming.

Take heart; God will lead you to the answers you are seeking. I'm reminded of an Os Guinness quote that hangs in my house: "We can't always know 'Why?', but we can always trust the one who knows why."

The ultimate Who behind the why is, of course, God. That patient endurance which Paul talks about can produce an abiding faith in the God who knows why, and it's that kind of faith that's necessary to carry on. This is where the experience of a sending agency comes in… to serve and guide you to where God's leading. So before you consider the options before you, the first question to answer is with whom should you partner? A sending agency partners with you to provide needed direction and support as you answer all the other questions about the who, what, where, when, and how of your calling.

THE BENEFITS OF WORKING WITH A MISSIONS SENDING AGENCY

While it is true that there are many ways missionaries are seeking to serve around the world today, in most cases sending agencies have flexible structures that support the various ways these global workers are serving. The greatest benefit a sending agency provides to a missionary is the experience and insight of those who have gone before.

The specialized experience that sending agencies provide allows global workers to receive support and resources far above what most local churches are able to offer. Because they focus on the needs of many missionaries, they have systems in place for financial oversight and security, ongoing training, and crisis management. A sending agency becomes your dedicated partner and ally on the mission field, so you can stay focused on your ministry while facing the demands of cross-cultural ministry.

Perhaps the most valuable service missions sending agencies provide is the support of fellow missionaries and coworkers. Having other missionaries that can truly understand the third-culture challenges of missionary existence is a great blessing in the work. They can come alongside you with peer support, coaching, and mentoring in the difficult moments you'll face. By facilitating gatherings with coworker from around the world and offering help through experienced missionaries who have been there—done that, missions agencies are able to help you navigate seasons of difficulty and burnout.

CHOOSING A MISSIONS SENDING AGENCY

There are many different ways to get connected with missions organizations. Maybe one has been recommended to you by your church or a close friend who serves with the organization. Perhaps you have discovered an agency that is connected to a specific area of ministry that you feel called to. Those are all good starting points for exploring whom to partner with.

Once you have a few possible sending agencies, the next step is to evaluate them. You are seeking the kind of alignment that will lead to a lasting partnership and enhance the work God has called you to do, and the decision should not be taken lightly. Here are three things to consider as you choose a sending agency.

1. **Biblical Truth**

    Are your beliefs about the Bible in line with the ministry you're seeking to partner with? Specifically, do you share the same doctrinal beliefs and convictions, ones you will pass on in your disciple-making? It's easy to say Jesus and the gospel is all we need to form a partnership in ministry, but every agency has a statement of belief that its partners endorse. You'll want to make sure you are not only familiar with it, but also in full agreement as you move toward collaborating in ministry.

    Why does this matter? Two reasons. First, you do not want your sending organization to be Christian in name only. Second, harmony in this area means the enemy has one less tactic for destroying the good work that God wants to do in and through you, as well as in those you serve.

2. **Biblical Relationships**

    Are the "one anothers" we see in the Bible being practiced among the agency's workers? A great way to predict how an agency will relate to you is to observe how the people in that ministry relate to each other. Jesus said, "They will know you are my disciples if you love one another." Does the organization you're considering reflect that kind of love for one another? Is there an environment of support, transparency, and trust?

Why does it matter? Jesus said that the way we love one another is our witness to the world. It is what sets us apart and makes people want to learn more about Jesus.

3. **Biblical Mission**

Are you aware of how the agency seeks to makes disciples? Are their methods consistent with your own practice? Missional methods, passion, and style are all a part of the mix, and you'll want to find synergy between yourself and your sending agency.

Why does it matter? Because some of the sharpest disagreements in ministry happen in this area, and you will be more effective if you're on the same page.

Pursuing Biblical Truth, Biblical Relationships, and Biblical Mission is not a DIY (Do-It-Yourself) project. The Great Commission is a DIT (Do-It-Together) project and considering these factors will allow you to make your decision with confidence. It's one more way that God can lead you toward the right fit in missions, and it's an important next step in discerning your calling.

 DIGGING DEEPER

Questions to Consider

1. What are the values you'd like to see embodied in a sending agency?

2. In what ways would you like the agency to support you during your preparation for ministry and while you serve?

3. What sending agencies already partner with your church? What can you learn from your church's experience in working with them?

4. What is your next step toward partnering with an agency?

Scriptures to Consider

Psalm 96; Jeremiah 29:11–13; Romans 12:1–8; Philippians 2:1–4; Proverbs 21:31

CALLED: FROM VOID TO VISION

Growing up, Matt had no room for God in his life. Though he regularly attended church with his believing parents, to him Christianity was just an outdated list of do's and don'ts. He had no interest in establishing a relationship with Jesus, nor any ambition to share a gospel he didn't really believe.

The more worldly delights he tasted, though, the more Matt felt an exhausting emptiness inside. He began to wonder if Jesus might hold some answers after all. A friend suggested he read C. S. Lewis's *Mere Christianity*, and as he did, one statement grabbed hold of Matt's heart: "If I find in myself desires which nothing in this world can satisfy, the only logical explanation is that I was made for another world." As he read those words, for the first time in his life, Matt understood the gospel.

A few months later, he prayed for God to claim him.

As he grew in his affection for Christ, Matt studied the Bible as much as he could. He quickly became convicted by passages like Luke 9:62, which says, "No one who puts his hand to the plow and looks back is fit for the kingdom of God." It was clear to him that God was demanding everything, and Matt began to think strongly about what he was going to do with the rest of his life.

Matt's idea of the missionary life was skewed. In his understanding, missionaries were people who do humanitarian initiatives in the jungle, get malaria, and have kids who are awkward when they come back to the States. He hoped God would never call him to that life. Then a missionary from Papua New Guinea visited his church, and his excellent presentation changed Matt's understanding of global missions and piqued his personal interest.

Looking for a place to begin, Matt researched missions organizations that offered short-term trips, and he found an internship with a team in Sweden. For three months, Matt interned with a church planting group in Stockholm that reached out to immigrants and refugees. The trip broadened his global perspective and cross-cultural understanding, which furthered his missional heart.

It also planted in his heart the desire to pursue unreached people groups.

Matt had an incredible time preaching the gospel in Stockholm, but for the first time, he wondered if he would be better utilized in a place where there was no church to proclaim the good news. Matt became certain that God was calling him to pursue unreached peoples.

Matt's initial research into opportunities to become a full-time vocational missionary led him to a mission in India. At first things looked great, but God unexpectedly closed that door. Matt was discouraged, and for a time, he put his future on hold while he waited for God to give him direction.

In the meantime, Matt moved to Los Angeles to help his friend with a church plant. He continued to research countries and people groups through the Joshua Project resource, and his days were marked with extensive time in prayer. After this time of preparation, God brought to light a country that had never before caught Matt's attention.

In 2011, an earthquake and tsunami decimated hundreds of Japanese cities.

As Matt watched the global news reports on the crisis in Japan, he wondered about God's eternal purpose for the tragic event. God began dropping Japan in Matt's lap everywhere he went. Matt got the hint. He started to research the need for the gospel in Japan, and as he read, he was shocked that he had never considered Japan before. It was a perfect fit for what he wanted to do in ministry.

God providentially connected Matt to a couple who were raising support to go to Japan, and they introduced Matt to Encompass and invited him to join in their vision to see Japan become a sending nation. He also met Encompass staff member Cecil O'Dell, who works with Japanese returnees in Long Beach, California. Matt became a part of Cecil's team as a way to prepare for future ministry in Japan.

As Matt looks back on his missional journey, he is amazed at how gracious God has been in his provision and direction. From being unsatisfied with what the world offers to being energized by a joyous vision for Japan, Matt is an example of how God fills his people and sends them out overflowing with the good news of his Son.

CONCLUSION

NEXT STEPS ON THE PATH

"Only one life, 'twill soon be past. Only what's done for Christ will last."

C. T. Studd

Thanks for engaging in the discernment journey through the learning, reflection, and guidance we've offered throughout this book. When I pray for people who are seeking God's calling for missions, I often quote David's words from Psalm 23—I pray that God will guide you "along the right paths for his name's sake." It is my great hope that God will lead you to a place of clarity in your calling, and that the gifts he has graced you with will be used to bring glory to him for all eternity. As is so eloquently stated by Paul to the Ephesians,

> *Now to him who is able to do far more abundantly than all that we ask or think, according to the power at work within us, to him be glory in the church and in Christ Jesus throughout all generations, forever and ever. Amen.*

Ephesians 3:20, 21

As I've shared before, the mobilization team at Encompass is here to serve as a guide as you seek the right fit in cross-cultural ministry. Together with the local church, we seek to partner to send workers into the harvest.

For more information, visit **EncompassWorldPartners.org/GO**.

NAVIGATE THE JOURNEY TO GLOBAL MISSIONS

Just as travel tools and resources guide you to destinations, give you insights, and point the way, the books in *The Path Series* will help you explore your calling and navigate the journey to global missions.

Mobilizing the Mobilizers
EQUIP AND RELEASE A MOBILIZATION TEAM
DAVE GUILES

Discerning Your Calling
DISCOVER YOUR PLACE AS A GLOBAL WORKER
JOHN WARD

Discovering Global Missions
EXPLORE GOD'S HEART FOR THE NATIONS
DAVE GUILES

MAP

GUIDE

COMPASS

Learn more and purchase online // PATHSERIES.COM

Made in the USA
Middletown, DE
03 October 2021

49537373R00040